*Zen Master Raven*

# ZEN MASTER RAVEN

## THE TEACHINGS OF A WISE OLD BIRD

COMPILED AND ANNOTATED BY

ROBERT AITKEN

WITH A NEW FOREWORD BY NELSON FOSTER

ILLUSTRATIONS BY JENNIFER RAIN CROSBY

Wisdom Publications
199 Elm Street
Somerville, MA 02144 USA
wisdompubs.org

An excerpt from this book appeared in *The International Journal of Transpersonal Studies*, vol. 19 (2000). Earlier versions of some of the cases appeared in *Mind Moon Circle* and *News from Kaimu.*

*Library of Congress Cataloging-in-Publication Data*
Names: Aitken, Robert, 1917–2010, author.
Title: Zen master raven: the teachings of a wise old bird / compiled and annotated by Robert Aitken; with a new foreword by Nelson Foster; illustrations by Jennifer Rain Crosby.
Description: Boston: Wisdom Publications, 2017. | Previously published: 2002.
Identifiers: LCCN 2016044504 (print) | LCCN 2017003502 (ebook) | ISBN 9781614293842 (hardback) | ISBN 1614293848 (hardback) | ISBN 9781614294009 (ebook) | ISBN 1614294003 (ebook)
Subjects: LCSH: Spiritual life—Zen Buddhism. | Zen Buddhism—Doctrines. | BISAC: RELIGION / Buddhism / Zen (see also PHILOSOPHY / Zen). | PHILOSOPHY / Zen. | HUMOR / Topic / Religion.
Classification: LCC BQ9386.2 .A38 2017 (print) | LCC BQ9386.2 (ebook) | DDC 294.3/927—dc23
LC record available at https://lccn.loc.gov/2016044504

ISBN 978-1-61429-384-2      ebook ISBN 978-1-61429-400-9

21 20 19 18 17
5  4  3  2  1

Cover design by Phil Pascuzzo. Interior design by Tony Lulek. Set in Arno Pro 11.5/16.75.

Wisdom Publications' books are printed on acid-free paper and meet the guidelines for permanence and durability of the Production Guidelines for Book Longevity of the Council on Library Resources.

This book was produced with environmental mindfulness. For more information, please visit wisdompubs.org/wisdom-environment.

Printed in the United States of America..

*For Tom Aitken*

# CONTENTS

# FOREWORD
*The Raven's Sources*

*Zen Master Raven* belongs, in a quirky sort of way, to a thousand-year-old literary tradition within the immense archives of Ch'an and Zen writings. Called *yü-lu* in Chinese or *goroku* in Japanese, such texts present themselves as life histories of great masters but ignore virtually all that contemporary biographies emphasize, reporting nothing of their subjects' childhood traumas, mature personalities, family conflicts, social stature, tastes, politics, or peccadilloes and seldom even describing their looks or habits. Instead, these accounts confine themselves almost exclusively to brief, freestanding dialogues (thus the term *yü-lu*, "discourse records") that the masters are purported to have had in the course of their careers.

I say "purported" since scholarship shows that, with very rare exceptions, few of the early records appeared until decades, often centuries, after their subjects had died and bear telltale signs of being cobbled together, if not altogether invented, in order to buff up the reputations of the ancestral teachers and boost the fortunes of their living successors. Nonetheless, generation upon generation of practitioners have held those *yü-lu* in the highest esteem, as documents truly exemplifying the masters' teachings and as standards of awakening. From them, especially the ones attributed to famous figures like Ma-tsu (Baso), Tung-shan (Tōzan), Yun-men (Unmon), Huang-po (Ōbaku), Chao-chou (Jōshū), and Lin-chi (Rinzai), come virtually all the classical kōans studied in Zen circles and now known far and wide.

In adopting the *yü-lu* format for his book, Robert Aitken— Aitken Rōshi, as he was fondly known to his students—laid unequivocal claim to this heritage, yet by setting it in the forest and assigning its dialogues to birds and beasts, at the same time he opened up an ironic and humorous distance from Zen tradition. Clearly he wanted it both ways, and I advise you to read it both ways: simultaneously as a serious record of his six decades practicing and eventually teaching Zen and as a lark, a merry improvisation by an old man living in retirement, entertaining himself and fully intending to entertain others as he set forth the path of liberation. The subtitle he gave the first edition neatly suited and signaled his thoroughly and happily mixed purposes: *Sayings and Doings of a Wise Bird*. See the gleam in his eye?

As a collaborator in the book's preparation, I know for certain that Aitken Rōshi incorporated into its pages exchanges (J., *mondō*, "questions-and-answers") that he'd had with others over the years. Certainly he edited the repartee as he transferred it from lips to beak or muzzle, masking the participants' identities and exercising poetic license to sharpen a point or improve phrasing. Some of Raven's snappy comebacks undoubtedly qualify as afterthoughts, too, and Aitken Rōshi may have dreamt up whole dialogues on his own. All the same, *Zen Master Raven* unquestionably deserves classification as a true discourse record. While obviously forgoing any pretense of strict factuality, it faithfully presents the substance of Aitken Rōshi's teaching and preserves the kind of direct give-and-take that he achieved with students at his best and that he considered crucial to Zen tradition. At the least, since every word of it came from his own hand, its origins are far more certifiable than the origins of records attributed to foundational Chinese masters.

As fresh and cohesive as its prose became, the book had a complex, two-decade-long process of gestation and development. Raven Rōshi himself didn't spring to life fully fledged; in fact he didn't even begin life as bird. Initially, Aitken Rōshi tried out wily Coyote as his animal alter ego, writing under the inspiration of Native American tales he'd heard during visits to Ring of Bone Zendo in the Sierra Nevada foothills. The first five dialogues to appear in print he billed as "Excerpts from Coyote Rōshi Goroku" and published in a 1982 issue of the San Francisco literary magazine *Coyote's Journal*. But these carry not a whiff of wild dog. Coyote seems merely to have lent his name to a two-legged Zen master easily identifiable as the author:

> Everybody knows how Coyote Rōshi loves to collect Buddhist images. Once a disciple of Rajneesh wrote to him, saying, "You are always looking for wooden Buddhas. You should come to India and meet a living Buddha."
>
> Coyote mentioned this letter to his students and remarked, "Living Buddhas are all over the place, but a good wooden Buddha is hard to find."

The other four exchanges in this sequence are similarly spare, lacking details to situate them in the forest and naming no animals besides Coyote. People close to Aitken Rōshi recognized some of the humans represented, including the former member of the Maui Zendo community who'd urged him to go to India and meet Rajneesh.

Seventeen years later, retired to an airy, oceanside home on the island of Hawai'i, Aitken Rōshi returned to the idea of writing up his record in Coyote-ized form, thinking it might plausibly expand to book length. As the work progressed, he began to introduce a few additional animal characters, notably a certain Dingo Rōshi, playing the important part of Coyote's principal teacher. In August 1999, debuting a selection of the dialogues in a quarterly miscellany of his recent news and writings, Aitken Rōshi described it as "a whimsy" and called it "Sayings and Doings of Zen Master Coyote." The seeking-Buddhas story remained intact except that the real-life Rajneesh had morphed into Rhino Rōshi. (When the book came out, a further revision made him Yogi Rhino.)

Meanwhile, Aitken Rōshi had sent the full manuscript to Gary Snyder, celebrated writer and founder of Ring of Bone Zendo, hoping that he'd provide an introduction for this new book, as he had for the earlier *Taking the Path of Zen*. In a postcard, declining, Snyder remarked, "Good luck with Coyote—he's tricky." Failing to register this caution or at least to heed it, for several more months Aitken Rōshi continued to circulate cases that featured Coyote as his stand-in. It became clear that he'd identified with just one aspect of Coyote's multifaceted persona—his knack for sly, often hilarious subversion of human preoccupations—while overlooking other qualities that made him a problematic proxy in the Zen woods. Coyote might have been an apt choice for a forthrightly unconventional figure like the fifteenth-century master Ikkyū, but for a proper gentleman like Aitken Rōshi, he made a poor fit.

In early 2000, abandoning Coyote as his mouthpiece, Aitken Rōshi picked Raven from a list of possible alternatives and set to work, with swiftly growing enthusiasm, to develop his personality and conjure other members of what soon became the Tallspruce Community. Here the record gained a further sort of authenticity, as the creative process stimulated Aitken Rōshi's memory of talking creatures he'd come to know over his many years of ardent reading. Aesop's fables, the Grimms' fairy tales, *Wind in the Willows, Alice in Wonderland*, Uncle Remus stories, *Charlotte's Web*, the rollicking Chinese Buddhist novel *Monkey*—these and other sources inspired his growing band of animal characters. So did Japanese ink paintings of well-attired frogs and rabbits, caricaturing priests and samurai, and a Tibetan Buddhist text he learned of only as he worked, *The Buddha's Law Among the Birds*, in which Avalokiteshvara, the bodhisattva of compassion, assumes the form of a cuckoo to instruct other birds in the Dharma. As the manuscript swelled with life, his writing grew frisky, and the forest population clarified, shedding species incongruous in a North American mix. Move over, Dingo Rōshi—here comes Brown Bear!

Reactions to the new work varied considerably. Aitken Rōshi's local students and visitors chuckled over the emerging stories and equally, perhaps, over their old teacher's boyish delight in sharing them. His son Tom, a next-door neighbor and school counselor, surprised him by greeting the book-in-progress with unusual excitement, predicting that it would come to be regarded as his "enduring legacy." Similarly impressed, Sam Shapiro, a professor of psychology at the University of Hawai'i, sought and received permission to run a sizable group of the Tallspruce tales in the 2000 issue of the *International Journal of Transpersonal Studies*. (There for the first time, at Shapiro's suggestion, each dialogue bore its own heading, while the excerpts as a whole carried the title "Sayings and Doings of Zen Master Raven: A Fable in Progress.") Yet overshadowing this favorable reception was the response most important to Aitken Rōshi: Zen student, longtime friend, deeply trusted literary advisor, and publisher Jack Shoemaker rejected the manuscript.

Shoemaker's refusal of an earlier project had put an end to it for good, but this time, fortunately, other voices prevailed. Although discouraged, Aitken Rōshi asked his agent to shop the book around, and it was quickly picked up by Tuttle Publishing, a firm with considerable experience handling books related to Japanese culture, including two beloved volumes by Aitken Rōshi's first Zen teacher, Nyogen Senzaki. Tuttle management had the good sense to approve the witty and beautiful artwork that Jennifer Rain Crosby supplied to complement the text, and in 2002 *Zen Master Raven* at last took flight.

Its idiosyncratic blend of incisive Zen teaching and playfulness won the book a devoted audience. How many copies of the first edition Tuttle sold I don't know, but I do know readers who return to it year after year and a few who actually started practicing Zen at the instigation of its wise old bird. Of the fourteen titles Aitken Rōshi authored or coauthored before his death in 2010, at the age of ninety-three, I'm aware of none that's elicited as many translations. Today, Raven croaks in at least four languages—Spanish, Swedish, Dutch, and German. I'm happy to imagine that this second English edition, from Wisdom Publications, enhanced by additional artwork from Jennifer Crosby, will enable him to stay aloft for generations to come and perhaps ride the winds to other distant lands.

Hee-Jin Kim, a distinguished scholar of the life and writings of Dōgen Zenji, has forecast a remarkable future for *Zen Master Raven*. In a public endorsement he wrote, "Most certainly, many of these stories will someday in the future be incorporated into the anthologies of home-grown American koans." This generous appraisal may not hold, of course. Only time will tell whether American Zen has the vitality and staying power to produce genuine kōan collections and, if so, whether Aitken Rōshi's *mondō* will find any place in them. Dr. Kim's comment reminds us that these dialogues are kōan candidates, at the most—but even that is high praise.

Zen Master Raven dives from his branch in the Assembly Oak, eyes ablaze.

NELSON FOSTER is a Dharma heir of Aitken Rōshi and succeeded him as second master of the Honolulu Diamond Sangha in 1997. Today, he teaches mainly at Ring of Bone Zendo, conducting annual sesshin also for the East Rock Sangha and the Maui Zendo. He edited several of Aitken Rōshi's books and served as principal compiler and author (with Jack Shoemaker) of *The Roaring Stream: A New Zen Reader.*

# ZEN MASTER RAVEN

# Searching for a Master

When Raven was living near Jackrabbit Rōshi, he visited him frequently to inquire about the Way. One day he asked, "I hear that the Buddha Shākyamuni looked up from beneath the Bodhi tree and saw the morning star and announced his realization.[1] I get the feeling that something is missing from the story. What happened when he saw the star?"

Jackrabbit laid back his ears, closed his eyes, and said, "He realized the truth of mutually dependent arising."[2]

"Well," thought Raven, "Jackrabbit Rōshi seems to know his Buddhism, but maybe I'm not a Buddhist." So he flew off to see Prairie Dog Rōshi.

When he announced himself, Prairie Dog poked her head out of her burrow and blinked in the bright sunshine. Raven told her about his encounter with Jackrabbit Rōshi and asked, "What happened when the Buddha saw the morning star?"

Prairie Dog crawled out and stood erect. She crossed her paws on her chest, scanned the horizon briefly, and said, "He realized the underlying fact of oneness."[3]

"Well," thought Raven, "Prairie Dog Rōshi seems to know her metaphysics, but maybe I'm not a metaphysician." So he flew off to see Moose Rōshi and found him feeding on waterweed in the creek at Cedarford. Perching himself on a rock, he croaked for the Rōshi's attention. When Moose looked up, Raven told him about his encounters with Jackrabbit Rōshi and Prairie Dog Rōshi and asked, "What happened when the Buddha saw the morning star?"

Moose dipped his face in the creek again and came up munching. "Delicious waterweed," he said.

"Well," thought Raven, "that sounds more natural." He sat on the rock a moment, but Moose said nothing further and just went on feeding. "Okay," thought Raven, "maybe I'll come back, but for now I think I'll continue this pilgrimage." So he flew off to see Brown Bear Rōshi.

Announcing himself, he stood and waited outside the den. Brown Bear eventually emerged and squatted silently on his haunches. Raven told him how Jackrabbit Rōshi had said the Buddha Shākyamuni realized the truth of mutually dependent arising, how Prairie Dog Rōshi had said he had realized the underlying fact of oneness, and how Moose Rōshi just said "Delicious waterweed."

"What is your opinion, Rōshi?" asked Raven.

Brown Bear made a strange sound, and Raven couldn't tell whether it was a chuckle or a growl. Finally he spoke. "Something's still missing," he said. Raven waited respectfully, but the Rōshi remained silent.

"Well," thought Raven, "Brown Bear Rōshi seems to know about something. Maybe I should stick around for instruction."

# METAPHOR

As they got better acquainted, Raven would ride on Brown Bear's back as he foraged for food. When they were setting out one day, Raven asked, "Do you teach exclusively with metaphor?"

Brown Bear said, "The robin sings in the oak tree; the finch sings in the madrone."

Raven asked, "What do they stand for?"

Brown Bear turned his head to look at Raven and asked, "The lark sings in the deep blue sky—what more can you ask?"[4]

Raven asked, "What is this singing?"

Brown Bear turned back to the path and grunted, "We'll have auditions again tonight."

# FAITH

One morning after a round of zazen,[5] Raven asked Brown Bear, "Does faith have a role in the practice?"

Brown Bear said, "Great faith."

Raven asked, "How should I direct it?"

Brown Bear said, "One, two, three."

# The Unborn

Relaxing with Brown Bear under the night sky, Raven asked, "What is the unborn?"

Brown Bear said, "Awesome."

Raven asked, "Is it the same thing as the void?"

Brown Bear asked, "Where does all this come from?"

# TURNING POINTS

Raven sat with Brown Bear at zazen early one morning, and afterward he asked, "Why don't we study turning points that are relevant for the forest today?"[6]

Brown Bear said, "Ask me a relevant question."

Raven asked, "Does the bear hunter have Buddha-nature?"

Brown Bear growled, "*Mu.*"[7]

"There you go," Raven said, "*Mu* is an old Asian word."

Brown Bear said, "That's the difficulty."

# Character

One evening, in a discussion of his personal problems, Raven asked Brown Bear, "What is the role of character in the practice?"

Brown Bear said, "I try to keep my promises."

Raven said, "I try to keep my promises, too, but I'm easily distracted."

Brown Bear said, "The cold wind reminds me."

# BIRTH AND DEATH

One evening after chanting sutras, Raven said, "Over at Jackrabbit Rōshi's community, we were taught that we should be free from birth and death. I've never known how to go about this."

Brown Bear said, "That's because it isn't possible."

Raven said, "There was a clear implication that it is."

Brown Bear lunged at Raven with a horrific snarl. Raven let out a croak and flew to a gray pine nearby.

Brown Bear looked up at him and asked, "What happened to make you croak?"

Raven hopped down to a lower perch and said, "I would rather ask the robin to explain."

Brown Bear sniffed and said, "Now the robin is taking over."

Raven said, "Only his beautiful song."

Brown Bear asked, "What happened to the stones and trees?"

Raven let out a croak.

Brown Bear asked, "Where did they go?"

Raven croaked and then croaked again.

Brown Bear nodded his big head slowly and showed his teeth at Raven. "The robin seems to have a bad cold this morning," he said finally, and both he and Raven laughed and laughed.

# THOROUGHGOING

Raven came to Brown Bear's den and walked right into his lair. "Time for me to be moving on," he announced.

Brown Bear asked, "What will you say about your study here?"

Raven said, "Brown Bear is quite thoroughgoing."

Brown Bear said, "Try camping out for a while."

# THE DREAM

Raven took Brown Bear's instruction to heart. He wandered a long time, from forests to upland meadows to icy lakes. Finally, with pinfeathers under his beak getting sparse, he found an abandoned place in a tall spruce tree. He fixed it up, and students began to gather, including Porcupine, who had studied with Coyote Rōshi. Other early students were Woodpecker, Grouse, Badger, Owl, and Black Bear, who lived nearby. They would sit in a circle in the little meadow under the tall spruce. Raven would sit with them and afterward would respond to their questions, and at more formal teaching times, he would take a perch in the outer branches of an oak tree close by—the Assembly Oak, as it came to be called. A stone outcropping served as an altar. One fine day Raven took his perch and said to the assembly: "We are children in the dream of the Buddha Shākyamuni.

He points to the center of our circle, and the King of the Gods sticks a blade of grass in the ground where he points. Our temple is established, and the Buddha smiles.[8] The bedrock heaved up from beneath the turf there on the far edge of our circle is his presence. We bow and chant his sutras with his throngs of followers down through the ages. His incense fills the air. His teaching gives us pause. Stop here with him."

The circle was silent. Finally Owl called out, "Are you sure that's not just your dream?"

Raven bobbed his head. "It is my dream."

# THE PIVOT

After zazen one evening Porcupine asked, "We examine turning points as our practice. What is the pivot on which this study turns?"

Raven said, "The large intestine."

Porcupine asked, "So, it's all physical?"

Raven said, "All physical, all mental, all moral, all spiritual, all void, all material."

Porcupine thought about this and finally asked, "What's the upshot?"

Raven said, "Trout in the pool, lilies on the bank."

# EGO

During one of the early gatherings at Tallspruce, Badger asked Raven, "How can I get rid of my ego?"

Raven said, "It's not strong enough."

"But I'm greedy," Badger said insistently. "I'm self-centered and I tend to push other folks around."

Raven said, "Like I said."

# THE SPIRIT OF THE PRACTICE

Relaxing with the others after zazen one evening, Owl asked, "What is the spirit of the practice?"

Raven said, "Inquiry."

Owl cocked his head and asked, "What do I inquire about?"

Raven said, "Good start."

# Timid and Truthful

Woodpecker appeared in the circle one warm summer evening with a guest. "This is Mole," she said. "He has life questions but is very timid about coming to meetings. He wants assurances that he is safe," and she cast a look at Badger and Owl.

Raven said, "Well, I'm a predator myself. It's good that we face this issue early." Addressing Mole, he said, "This is the Buddha's sacred temple, where his disciples from all over can feel safe together. You are safe here. Right, Owl? Right, Badger?"

"Safe here," they echoed.

Mole seemed to shiver, but he spoke up and said, "Thank you. I confess I still feel uneasy, but my questions make me stay. Funny situation, isn't it!"

Raven said, "Is there anything that isn't peculiar?"

Mole said nothing.

Raven said, "Anyway, do you want to ask something?"

Mole cleared his throat and asked, "Should I always tell the truth? Sometimes it does more harm than good."

Raven said, "Then it's not the truth."

Mole sighed and was silent.

Owl spoke up and asked, "Then should I lie at such a time?"

Raven said, "Tell the truth."

# ESSENTIAL NATURE

Early one morning Woodpecker flew in for a special meeting with Raven and asked, "I've heard about essential nature, but I'm not sure what it is. Is it something that can be destroyed?"

Raven said, "That's really a presumptuous question."

Woodpecker ruffled her feathers a little and asked, "You mean I shouldn't question the matter?"

Raven said, "You presume there is one."

# BEDROCK BUDDHA

Once a disciple of Yogi Rhino sent Raven a message, saying, "You just have a stone outcropping to represent the Buddha. You should come over here and meet a living Buddha."

Raven mentioned this in a talk and said, "If that fellow stays on with Yogi Rhino, he might realize that living Buddhas are all over the place, and yet our bedrock stands forth alone."

# INSPIRATION

Raven took his perch on the Assembly Oak and said, "Some folks say that you must find your inspiration in your own heart. In a way that's true; you must find the place of peace and rest and carry out your life on that ground.

"It is also true that inspiration comes from somewhere else. The Buddha looked up from his seat under the Bodhi tree and noticed the morning star. With that he had his great realization. What did he realize? That's what we have to get at.

"The Buddha gave a broad hint about his new understanding when he said, 'Now I see that all beings are the Buddha!'[9] All beings, all that exists, each and every thing, precious in itself, coming forth saying 'Here I am!'"

Grouse muttered something, and Raven said, "Grouse, did you have a question?"

Grouse said, "Here I am, but I don't think I'm so precious."

Raven said, "Cluck for us, Grouse." Grouse clucked. Raven croaked.

# KARMA

One evening Gray Wolf appeared in the Tallspruce circle for the first time. After she had introduced herself, she said, "Is it all right to ask a question?"

Raven said, "Not only all right."

"Thank you," said Gray Wolf. "Maybe it's obvious to everyone else, but I don't understand the notion of karma. Could you explain it to me?"

Raven said, "Murder will out."

Gray Wolf said, "Sometimes crimes are never solved."

Raven said, "Help me not to live a lie."

# PROPINQUITY

Cougar also came by that evening for the first time. After Raven's final response to Gray Wolf, he asked, "Then is karma just cause and effect?"

Raven said, "Propinquity propinks."

Cougar shook his head vigorously and said, "Sometimes it makes me irritated."

Raven said, "Your great chance."

# The Purpose of the Practice

Badger attended the circle irregularly because of family responsibilities. One evening he was able to come for zazen and questions. He asked, "What is the purpose of the practice after all?"

Raven asked, "Do you have an inkling?"

Badger hesitated. "I'm not sure," he said.

Raven said, "Doubts dig up the whole Blue Planet."

# BROWN BEAR'S PURPOSE

That same evening Porcupine asked, "What did Brown Bear have in mind when he took up his role as teacher?"[10]

Raven said, "To make little girls ask questions."

Porcupine said, "Don't patronize me, Rōshi. My question is: What did Brown Bear have in mind when he took up the role of teacher?"

Raven bobbed his head. "Excellent! Excellent!"

Porcupine stamped her foot. "That's not an answer!"

Raven said, "He didn't have answers in mind."

# BUDDHIST TERMS

After zazen one evening Woodpecker asked, "I'd like to understand basic Buddhist terms, but I'm not sure that would help my practice. What do you think?"

Raven said, "They help us sort out our vows."

Woodpecker asked, "Then they're a kind of appropriate means?"[11]

Raven said, "Like the rain."

# Maintenance

Mallard attended meetings for a while before asking her first question: "Aren't we wasting time just sitting here while the Blue Planet goes to hell?"

Raven asked, "Do you waste your time eating?"

"Is that all it is," Mallard asked, "just personal maintenance?"

Raven said, "Mallard maintenance, lake maintenance, juniper maintenance, deer maintenance."

# BUDDHA

The next evening Woodpecker spoke up and said, "I'd like to follow up on Buddhist terms. Let's start with the basic one. What is Buddha?"

Raven said, "I won't say."

"Oh, come on!" Woodpecker exclaimed.

Raven let out a croak and flew into the Assembly Oak.

# DELUSION

Another time Woodpecker asked, "What can you say about delusion?"

Raven said, "Juniper bush."

Woodpecker said, "How is the juniper bush a delusion?"

Raven said, "It shades me on a warm afternoon."

Woodpecker thought a moment and then asked, "Then naming things is delusion?"

Raven said, "Just so you know the risks."

# MYTHOLOGY

Raven took his students to see Stag Sensei, who taught karate at Bentpine. Stag gave a little talk and showed them some of the exercises. Then in the Founder's Glade they bowed before a large stone in the form of Bodhidharma.

Back home that evening, Porcupine asked, "Was Bodhidharma really the founder of karate?"[12]

Raven said, "That depends on your mythology."

Porcupine asked, "What is your mythology, Rōshi?"

Raven said, "I bow."

# ENLIGHTENMENT

One day when they were sitting around having a snack, Woodpecker asked Raven, "What is enlightenment?"

Raven said, "I won't deny it."

Woodpecker asked, "What will you affirm?"

Raven said, "Containment."

Woodpecker said, "What kind of containment?"

Raven asked, "What about you?"

Woodpecker hesitated.

Raven said, "The moon is not on the fringes."

# DEATH

Mole came to Raven privately and said, "We haven't talked about death very much. I'm not concerned about where I will go, but watching so many family members die, I'm wondering what happens at the point of death?"

Raven sat silently for a while, then said, "I give away my belongings."

# THE HOLY SPIRIT

Reverend Crane invited Raven and his students to an ecumenical service at the Little Church in the Grotto. Afterward the Tallspruce community was abuzz about the experience. The next evening Owl asked, "Is the Holy Spirit something like Buddha-nature?"

Raven said, "The two ideas are similar."

Owl asked, "Then Christianity and Zen are somehow linked?"

Raven said, "No, not at all, they are totally different and distinctly separate."

Owl was silent for a moment. Then he asked, "How are they different?"

Raven said, "Their ideas of idea are different."

Owl asked, "How are their ideas of idea different?"

Raven said, "One has eternal life, and the other expires before sunset."

# VERY SPECIAL

In a group munching grubs one afternoon, Mole remarked, "The Buddha Shākyamuni was very special, wasn't he! I'm sure there has never been anyone like him."

Raven said, "Like the madrone."

Mole asked, "How is the madrone unique?"

Raven said, "Every madrone leaf."

Mole fell silent.

Porcupine asked, "How does the uniqueness of every madrone leaf relate to the practice?"

Raven said, "Your practice."

# METAPHYSICS

That evening Owl said, "I'm still thinking about our experience at the Little Church in the Grotto. Can a Buddhist be a Christian?"

Raven said, "Love thy neighbor."

Owl asked, "Can a Christian be a Buddhist?"

Raven said, "There are lots of them."

Owl asked, "Aren't you bypassing a conflict in metaphysics?"

Raven asked, "What has metaphysics got to do with it?"

Owl asked, "What is the antecedent of *it*?"

Raven said, "Good move, Owl."

# First-Person Singular

Wolverine came by unannounced one evening in early autumn.

"Hello," said Raven, "I'm Raven."

Wolverine said, "The Rōshi is meeting this one for the first time."

Raven said, "Is that so? What happened to the first-person singular?"

Wolverine said, "No-self has appeared."

Raven said, "Could've fooled me."

# VENERATION AND WORSHIP

Woodpecker said, "I'm like Owl, still thinking about our visit to the Little Church in the Grotto. I wonder, what's the difference between veneration and worship?"

Raven said, "One makes your tummy warm, the other doesn't."

Woodpecker asked, "Which is which?"

Raven said, "Not my business."

# MAKE SENSE

One evening Raven took his perch on the Assembly Oak and said, "I worked with Jackrabbit Rōshi for a long time, and there were certain things in his teaching that troubled me. I never asked about them, and finally I just came to the end and left. I think now that if I had spoken up sooner, it might have helped us both. So now I would ask you, is there anything in our program that troubles you?"

There was a long silence. Finally Turkey, a visitor that evening, spoke up. "I've been wondering," she said, "why it is that you don't have more songbirds in your community."

Raven said, "Maybe they're content just to inspire us from the trees."

Turkey asked, "How can they be inspired?"

Raven said, "Make sense."

# THE NEW DISCUSSION LEADER

At the end of an evening meeting, Raven announced, "The Assembly Oak will preside tomorrow night."

Woodpecker said, "This I'll have to see."

Next night, Raven appeared at his usual place in the circle. Woodpecker said, "You said the Assembly Oak would preside tonight."

Raven said, "I'm here, but I've forgotten what I was going to say."

# GUIDELINES

Porcupine came by Tallspruce one day to see if she could just hang out with Raven. She found him in consultation with Woodpecker, so she made herself scarce until he was free. Then she said, "You're an experienced master now. Do you have a general set of guidelines for your teaching of the Way?"

Raven said, "Don't give away the nest."

Porcupine said, "You seem to be saying that you can only give hints."

Raven said, "I don't hint. I say it directly."

Porcupine said, "Okay, what is *Mu*?"

Raven said, "Stillpond is an analogy, not a metaphor."

Porcupine said, "What's the metaphor?"

Raven said, "No longer a stranger to your inheritance."

Porcupine said, "Doesn't sound so direct to me."

Raven said, "Okay, what is *Mu*?"

# DISCOURAGED

Grouse was looking rather moody one evening, and as the group was breaking up at the end of the meeting, Raven called to her, "Hey, Grouse! How's it going?"

"Oh," said Grouse, "I don't know. Sometimes I feel discouraged. Why is it that I'm taking so long to understand anything?"

Raven said, "Everybody takes the same length of time."

"There are folks who came after I did," said Grouse, shaking her head. "They ask intelligent questions and seem to be moving along in their practice while I just sit and sit and wonder what is going on."

Raven said, "They say the Buddha Shākyamuni is still sitting somewhere and he's only halfway."

Grouse said, "That's not very encouraging."

Raven said, "Come to think of it, it's not."

# OUTSIDE HISTORY

Badger had been busy again, looking after his family. One evening after his return, he asked, "Is there really something to understand beyond the way to be a better person?"

Raven said, "Outside history."

Badger asked, "In a vacuum?"

Raven said, "Where the freshet washed away the moss."

# THE DARK SIDE

Next day, Woodpecker came around when Raven was cleaning up after a windstorm and asked, "Do you think I could be a teacher?"

Raven looked her over. "What's the dark side?" he asked.

Woodpecker hesitated. "I'm not sure there is one," she said.

Raven turned away, saying, "Then how can you be a teacher?"

# THE GOOD OF PRACTICE

Grouse missed zazen one evening but came later to ask a question: "I'm hearing that some old-time students and even teachers act selfishly and cause dissension in the community. So what's the good of practice?"

Raven said, "It takes, or it doesn't take."

Grouse asked, "What does it take to take?"

Raven said, "Practice."

Grouse sighed and was silent.

Owl said, "I don't get it. If practice doesn't take, how will more practice do it?"

Raven said, "I hope I live long enough."

# Does the Way Have Feelings?

Badger was well liked in the community, and the folks were always glad to see him. One day he was able to come to zazen and the informal discussion afterward. Mole said, "I'm glad that you were able to come tonight. I know it's not easy for you to get away."

Badger said, "Thank you, Mole. It means a lot to me to be here and to practice the Way with everybody."

Raven said, "It means a lot to the Way, too."

Badger sat back and looked puzzled.

Owl spoke up and asked, "Does the Way have feelings?"

"Watch the ants," said Raven.

# RAVEN RŌSHI

One morning Porcupine came to Raven privately and asked, "What is Raven Rōshi?"

Raven said, "I have this urge to prey on newborn lambs."

Porcupine asked, "How do you deal with it?"

Raven said, "I'd be disoriented without it."

# THE WAY THINGS ARE

Raven took his perch on the Assembly Oak and said, "The problem is that one thing seems to lead to another."

Owl asked, "Isn't that the way things are?"

Raven said, "Not really."

Owl cocked his head. "You just said…," he began.

Raven croaked.

# Pain during Zazen

Black Bear came to see Raven one morning and said, "I have this persistent pain under my right shoulder blade. Shall I try sitting through it?"

Raven asked, "Have you tried sitting through it?"

Black Bear said, "It just gets worse."

Raven said, "Maybe you should elevate your seat a little. Try sitting on a stone."

Black Bear said, "It doesn't seem to help."

Raven said, "Try lying down."

Black Bear said, "Can I really do zazen lying down?"

Raven asked, "How else can you do it?"

# Zazen in the Forest

It had been stormy for several days, and the community did not meet. Finally, the winds calmed, the rains stopped, and the meetings resumed. Owl obviously wanted to speak, so the others deferred. "I've been told," he said, "that long ago, folks could devote themselves full-time to the practice, and enlightened masters emerged. Nowadays here in the forest, folks are so busy hunting and gleaning and protecting themselves that they have very little time for zazen. How can we hope to attain the level of realization the old masters attained?"

Raven said, "They saw plum blossoms; we hear the robin."

Owl said, "But it seems their very atmosphere was charged with realization. That's certainly not true for us today."

Raven said, "The robin just flew away."

# ORDINARY MORALITY

Porcupine came by one day looking troubled. Raven called down to her from the tall spruce. "What's up, Porcupine?"

Porcupine said, "I'm hearing rumors from my old friends that Coyote Rōshi is violating even ordinary morality."

Raven flew down to her side and said, "She has this urge to prey on newborn lambs."

Porcupine said, "You said that you have that same urge. Is it that you don't follow through?"

Raven said, "I am following through at this moment."

Porcupine asked, "How is talking to me following through with your urge to eat baby lambs?"

Raven said, "Use the urge."

# DREAMS

One afternoon, after the Tallspruce group hiked over to Lowridge for berries, Black Bear said to Raven, "This is my last get-together before I retire for the winter. There is something I want to ask. I dream a lot when I'm hibernating—do Zen masters dream?"

Raven said, "Higgledy-piggledy."

Black Bear chuckled. "My dreams are like that, too—all confused!"

Raven said, "Not only our dreams."

Black Bear asked, "Then how can Zen masters be distinguished?"

Raven stretched out his wings.

# Open and Clear

Porcupine came to Raven for a special interview and said, "Last night when I was putting little Porky to bed, I suddenly realized that everything is completely open and clear to the very bottom."

Raven asked, "What about you?"

Porcupine was silent.

# THE MIND

One evening Owl said, "I've heard that the mind is the mountains, the rivers, and the great Blue Planet."[13]

Raven said, "Right."

Owl continued, "And that the mind is neither tall nor short."[14]

Raven said, "That, too."

Owl asked, "Then what is the mind?"

Raven said, "Beans."

# SUFFERING

Winter set in firmly, and frequent snowstorms prevented the community from meeting. One day was unseasonably warm, however, and a few members gathered for a day of zazen. In the question period, Owl said, "Many folks aren't surviving the winter, and I think all of us are reminded that we won't be here long. I'm not sure what my question is, but ..." His voice trailed off.

Raven said, "Maybe there isn't a question."

Mole spoke up and said, "I think there is. There's a lot of suffering in this forest. Folks are dying and leaving little ones with no one to care for them; folks get sick; they get killed and eaten. How does this fit the teaching of the Buddha?"

Raven said, "He was concerned about the misery of suffering."

Mole asked, "Is there suffering without misery?"

Raven said, "Yours—right now."

Mole was silent.

Owl asked, "So the teaching of the Buddha was really just to grin and bear it?"

Raven jumped up and down, chanting, "Getting old! Getting old!" and he gave a great croak.

# Panic and Fear

Porcupine came again to Raven for a special interview and said, "A week ago I found that everything was completely open and clear to the very bottom, but last night I woke up for no reason and was filled with fear and panic. What's going on?"

Raven said, "A week ago you realized that everything is completely open and clear to the very bottom, and last night you woke up filled with fear and panic."

Porcupine hung her head and asked, "What should I do?"

Raven said, "The context is not the practice."

Porcupine thought for a moment and said, "I should think the context *is* the practice."

Raven bobbed his head. "It is, it is, make no mistake."

"You just said it isn't," Porcupine protested.

Raven said, "The context is the practice because your body and mind are engaged, not to mention cedars and the wind. It is not the practice because it is not your focus."

# The Eightfold Path

Spring finally came, and Raven entertained his old teacher Brown Bear Rōshi and invited him to speak. After the talk, Badger came forward and asked, "How can I get rid of my passions?"

Brown Bear said, "What would you be without passions?"

Badger said, "Maybe I should reword that. How can I get rid of my attachments?"

Brown Bear said, "What would you be without attachments?"

Badger said, "Isn't nonattachment one of our ideals?"

Brown Bear asked, "Where do you find it taught?"

Badger said, "Isn't it implicit in the Eightfold Path of the Buddha?"[15]

Brown Bear said, "Cling to that Path."

Raven commented, "I'm clinging to Brown Bear."

# RIGHT VIEWS

Owl then spoke up and asked, "What is the essential point of the Eightfold Path?"

Brown Bear said, "It goes around and around."

Owl drew back his head and exclaimed, "Really? I thought it was a linear path. And I've always thought there should be a ninth step—that Right Realization should come after Right Zazen."

Brown Bear said, "Right Views come after Right Zazen."

Owl said, "Then where does Right Realization come in?"

Brown Bear said, "Right Views! Right Views!"

Owl said, "What are Right Views?"

Brown Bear said, "We're in it together, and we don't have much time."

# RIGHT THINKING

Later in the same meeting, Owl then asked another question: "Right Thinking comes immediately after Right Views. I have problems with my thinking. What is Right Thinking?"

Brown Bear said, "The point."

Owl said, "My thoughts go on and on."

Brown Bear asked, "Is that your focus?"

Owl blinked and said nothing.

# PATIENCE

Gray Wolf attended meetings sporadically, and when she came she usually sat silent during the question period. However, she came to hear Brown Bear and spoke up, saying, "We dedicate our sutras to the enlightenment of bushes and grasses. This doesn't seem so likely somehow."[16]

Brown Bear chuckled and said, "They are very patient."

# DELINEATION

Porcupine came over with a gift of leavings. "Kind of you," said Raven.

"I have a report," said Porcupine. "This morning when the birds woke me up, I realized that my quills and my skin don't delineate me."

"What delineates you?" asked Raven.

"You always blink when you ask a hard question," said Porcupine.

Raven said, "You are very observant."

# SAVING THE MANY BEINGS

Mallard appeared in the circle after a trip and asked, "The first of our vows is to save the many beings.[17] You told us that the Sixth Ancestor said this means 'You save them in your own mind.'[18] Is that all there is to fulfilling this vow?"

Raven said, "Completely fulfilled."

Mallard said, "But what then?"

Raven said, "Not just your skull."

# EMPTINESS

At a Tallspruce party, Porcupine cornered Raven and said, "I wanted to tell you that I've found that there is no basis for emptiness."

Raven looked startled; then he and Porcupine burst into laughter.

# THE STICK

Grandma had been living at Vinecot for as long as anyone could remember. She was white-haired and bent, and she walked with a stick. She lived quietly but was a good friend of Turkey, who had free run of her house. One day she came to see Raven, who promptly flew up into the Assembly Oak. "Come down here, Raven Rōshi," she said, "I want to talk to you."

Raven flew down before her and said, "Turkey and others have told me that you know our language, but I'm surprised at how well you speak it."

"Oh," said Grandma, "I've been living in the forest for a while. I just pay attention to what I hear. There's a certain frequency…"

"For us, too," said Raven.

Grandma said, "Oh yes, that makes sense. But I didn't come to see you to gossip about communication."

Raven drew himself up. "I'm forgetting my manners," he said, bowing. "I'm pleased to meet you. You have come quite a long way. To what do I owe the honor of this visit?"

Grandma held out her stick and said, "I just wanted to ask you what this is."

Raven let out a croak and flew at the stick. Grandma pulled it away and said, "It's mine. You can't have it."

Raven said, "Is that so? I see. I see."

# CAN'T HAVE THAT

That evening Raven took his perch and said to the assembly, "Grandma came to see me today. She held out her stick and asked me what it was. I went to take it in my talons, but she pulled it away and said, 'It's mine. You can't have it.' How would you respond if she asked you what it is?"

The assembly was silent. Porcupine curled up and raised her spines.

Raven said, "Can't have that, either."

# HOW DO YOU ACCOUNT FOR THIS?

At that same assembly, Mole said to Raven, "Turkey tells me that Grandma doesn't lock her place and that folks are free to wander in and out. They eat her food and mess up her carpet. She doesn't seem to be protective or possessive at all. Yet she snatched away her stick when you went after it. How do you account for this?"

Raven said, "It guides her along to Vinecot on a moonless night. It helps her cross the creek when the bridge is broken down."[19]

Mole subsided.

After a moment, Woodpecker asked, "You mean when push comes to shove, there are certain things that she won't share?"

Raven said, "Stick."

# TOO CLEVER BY HALF

Owl then spoke up. "Are you saying that her stick represents her Buddha-nature?"

Raven launched himself from his perch without a word and flew out of sight.

Porcupine said, "Don't you see? It's a plain old stick. It doesn't even have a rubber tip."

Owl said, "Sometimes I think I'm just too clever by half."

# Not Playing Favorites

Woodpecker flew over to Vinecot, and there was the stick leaning against the corner of the porch. She called out, "Hello! Hello!"

Grandma came to the door.

Woodpecker said, "Is that your stick?"

Grandma said, "You can take it away with you if you like."

Woodpecker said, "I heard that you wouldn't give it to Raven."

Grandma said, "I still wouldn't."

Woodpecker then flew back to Raven and said, "I went to see Grandma and she offered to let me have her stick. I told her I had heard that she wouldn't give it to you, and she said she still wouldn't. Surely she's not playing favorites."

Raven said, "For pine nuts go to the pine tree."

# THE FUN WAY

Next evening, Porcupine said, "I think I speak for everyone in suggesting that we invite Grandma to our meetings. She's quite wise, it seems."

Raven saw many heads nodding. The next day he flew over to Vinecot and found Grandma weeding her garden. "We'd like to invite you to come to our meetings," he said.

Grandma said, "It's much more fun this way."

Raven said, "Might have known."

# ZAZEN ALONE

Mallard spoke up first at an evening meeting and said, "When I'm traveling, I find it difficult to do zazen without support from the community. As often as not, I end up not doing it."

Raven said, "Sit with the stones."

# PERSPECTIVE

Woodpecker said, "You've told us how Jackrabbit Rōshi said that when the Buddha looked up and saw the morning star, he realized the truth of mutually dependent arising. I hear that the Rōshi is now saying that the Buddha realized 'Just this!'"

Raven said, "Something's still missing."

"But isn't that what the Buddha realized?" asked Woodpecker, "'Just this morning star'?"

Raven ruffled his feathers and said, "No."

Later, Woodpecker asked Porcupine about this. Porcupine said, "Something's still prevailing."

Woodpecker returned to Raven and said, "I'm trying to get

to the bottom of this case about the morning star. You said, 'Something's still missing.' Porcupine said, 'Something's still prevailing.' I really don't understand."

Raven said, "Porcupine adds perspective."

# NOT HELPING

After a talk by Raven about the precepts, Woodpecker said, "The cowbird lays her egg in the wren's nest, and the two wrens have to hustle to feed the cowbird's baby as well as their own. I don't see why the wrens stand for it, especially since the cowbird's baby is a lot bigger than theirs and has a huge appetite. Maybe the wrens are really bodhisattvas, selflessly devoted to helping others."

Raven said, "They aren't helping the cowbirds."

# MOSQUITO

One night after a meeting, the Tallspruce community lingered in the dark under the stars, and Raven reminisced about his time with Brown Bear. "I remember," he said, "one day when I wasn't feeling well, and Brown Bear Rōshi had me rest in his cave. Somehow it was a special gathering place for mosquitoes. One of them suspended herself before my face. She was almost not there—so fragile, her long, thread-like legs hanging down motionless. I marveled that she was a living being with appetites and incentive, yet hardly more than gossamer.

"In our sutras we chant the lines 'Forms are no other than emptiness; emptiness no other than forms.'[20] Sometime earlier, when I was looking up at the night sky, I thought I understood that passage, but when I was resting in Brown Bear's lair and I felt that mosquito sink her long proboscis into my face, I was at last able to appreciate the mystery."

# FOLLOW YOUR BLISS

Grandma was chatting with Turkey at Vinecot, when Granddaughter made a surprise visit. That evening after supper, when they had caught up with each other's news, Granddaughter said, "Now that I've finished school, I don't know what I will do next."

Grandma said, "Follow your bliss."

Granddaughter said, "That sounds selfish."

Grandma said, "Your employers don't all have desks and files."

Next evening, Turkey asked Raven about Grandma's advice. Raven said, "It's like Brown Bear said: 'The robin sings in the oak tree; the finch sings in the madrone.'" Turkey did not respond.

Woodpecker asked, "Aren't they distractions?"

Raven asked, "From what?"

Turkey seemed to come to herself, and gobbled.

Raven said, "Like that."

# He Doesn't Know

Once a visitor asked Brown Bear, "What is the meaning of the passage 'Forms are no other than emptiness'?"

Brown Bear said, "I don't know; it's from an old sutra."

Raven took his perch one evening and repeated this story.

Owl asked, "Brown Bear Rōshi knows the sutras very well. How could he say he didn't know?"

Raven said, "He doesn't know."

Owl said, "But he's a great teacher. He's our grandfather in the Great Law."

Raven said, "He really doesn't know."

# VOWS

Gray Wolf seemed to attend meetings against her better judgment. One evening she came by anyway and said, "In every service I renew my vow to save the many beings, but, really, how can I do that?"

Raven said, "It's your precious keepsake."

Mallard asked, "How can a vow be a keepsake?"

Raven said, "It reminds you of a loved one."

Gray Wolf sat back and said nothing further.

Owl spoke up and said, "We also vow to waken to the countless gates of the Great Law.[21] I always thought that vow meant I should study all the various Buddhist teachings, but now I'm not so sure."

Raven said, "See all the new green leaves glittering in the sunshine!"[22]

# GOSSIP

Porcupine was leading an orientation to the practice when Mockingbird dropped in. During the question period she said, "I have a tendency to gossip. I know it can be hurtful, yet I can't seem to stop."

Porcupine said, "It's fun."

Mockingbird said, "Yes, but at the expense of others."

Porcupine said, "Dirt is dirt!"

# ANGER

When the community was discussing ethics after zazen one evening, Black Bear remarked, "I have a hard time dealing with my anger."

Raven said, "Check it out afterward."

Black Bear said, "What good will that do?"

Raven said, "It might have been Great Bear's anger."

# GIVING

Grouse spoke up at a gathering and asked, "Mole said that a while back you said that you give away your belongings when you die. I've been brooding about this, but it still isn't clear to me."

Raven said, "What isn't clear?"

Grouse asked, "Is there anything left?"

Raven said, "Oh lots: the moon, the wind, the crickets."

# THE MIDDLE WAY

One evening Woodpecker asked, "What is the Middle Way?"[23]

Raven said, "Good question."

Woodpecker said, "You're dodging my question."

Raven said, "You're dodging my answer."

# READING

Granddaughter asked Grandma, "I've heard that some Zen teachers advise their students not to read. What is your opinion?"

Grandma said, "Read."

Granddaughter asked, "What should I read?"

Grandma said, "Watch for your name."

Turkey told Raven about this. Raven asked, "How is that for you?"

Turkey said, "Dunno, Rōshi. Books don't mean much to me."

Raven said, "You have your own works."

# ESSENTIAL

One evening during the question period, Owl asked Raven, "How important are the words of the Buddha and his successors to our practice?"

Raven said, "Essential."

"Is there anything more essential?" asked Owl.

Raven said, "The bullfrog calls his mate."

Owl was silent but did not return to his place in the circle.

Raven continued, "You see, Owl, the Buddha explains it."

Owl asked, "What does he explain?"

Raven cawed.

# STILL LONESOME

Mole spoke up after Raven had his exchange with Owl and said, "I have a different kind of question. Is there a way to practice in ordinary times?"

Raven said, "The robin! The dove! The linnet!"

"Is it just a matter of being open to the other?" asked Mole.

"Still lonesome," said Raven.

# TOO BUSY

Owl said, "I notice that some students go from teacher to teacher. What do you think of this?"

Raven said, "Busy."

"After all," Owl said, "practice is a matter of settling in."

Raven said, "Still too busy."

Owl said nothing.

# TRUST

Porcupine then asked, "Is trust in the teacher important for the practice?"

Raven said, "Indispensable."

Porcupine asked, "Can't that create problems?"

Raven said, "Interminable."

# The Self

Badger came to Raven privately and asked, "What is the self?"
Raven said, "Passion."

Badger asked, "Why are we told to forget it?"

Raven said, "Forget it!"

Badger said, "That's scary."

Raven croaked. Badger sat back on his haunches and was silent.

Raven said, "Now I'm tired."

# THE ESSENCE

One evening Owl asked, "I've heard that Jackrabbit Rōshi said that the mind has no qualities and its essence is compassion. What do you think of that?"

Raven said, "The mind is compassion and its essence has no qualities."

# HEARING

Raven took his perch and said, "Things just come in. Do you listen, or do you hear? When you listen, you are paying attention to something out there, but when you hear, the sounds just come in. You are sitting there with your ears open, and the dove calls out. That sound defines you. Once you are defined like that, the cedars can define you, the faraway skunk can define you."

Woodpecker asked, "Is that realization?"

Raven said, "Let yourself hear the dove."

# UNHAPPY

Raven met Grouse moping around one day and asked, "How's it going, Grouse?"

Grouse said, "I'm so unhappy."

Raven said, "What do you think might make you happy?"

Grouse said, "I don't know. I don't ask for much."

Raven said, "Way too much."

# HONESTY

Black Bear came to a meeting late and said, "I'm feeling frazzled after dealing with my cubs. What if I don't feel compassionate?"

Raven said, "Fake it."

"That doesn't seem honest," said Black Bear.

"It doesn't begin with honesty," said Raven.

# METHOD

Porcupine began special consultations with Raven. One day she asked, "What is your method?"

Raven said, "Evident."

Porcupine said, "You purvey the obvious?"

Raven said, "Stick kernels in every cranny."[24]

# BLASPHEMY

One evening Woodpecker asked, "What is blasphemy?" Raven said, "The Buddha Shākyamuni was perfectly enlightened."

# ATTAINMENT

That same evening Owl said, "I've heard that you should not try to attain anything. What do you think?"

Raven said, "Not attain anything? Then what are you doing here?"

Owl said, "I think the idea is that we're Buddhas already, so there's nothing to attain."

Raven said, "An attained being said that."

# THE PERFECTION OF CHARACTER

Raccoon was a student of Moose Rōshi at Cedarford, but he visited the Tallspruce community occasionally. One day Raven invited him to have a snack and asked, "What does Moose Rōshi teach?"

Raccoon said, "The practice of Zen is the perfection of character."

Raven said, "Transformation."

Raccoon said, "How can Zen bring transformation?"

Raven said, "The Zen student trims the dead branches. It's the pigeon who can do the actual job."

# INTIMATE

One evening Badger asked, "What's realization like?" Raven said, "Intimate."

Badger asked, "Can you share it?"

Raven said, "Where have you *been?*" Fluffing his feathers, he turned away, muttering to himself, "Ah, such as it is."

# WHAT IS MIND?

Sitting around after supper one night, Granddaughter looked up from a book she was reading and asked, "What is mind?"

Grandma said, "Kitty is crying for food."

Granddaughter asked, "Do you mean anything will do?"

Grandma said, "No."

Granddaughter waited for more, but Grandma had returned to her knitting. She sighed and got up to feed the cat.

Later, Turkey reported this to Raven and asked his opinion. Raven croaked, and then croaked again.

Turkey asked, "Will that do it?"

Raven said, "Apparently not."

# CONFINED

Badger spoke up after a long silence one evening and asked, "Is there a power outside myself?"

Raven said, "Confined."

"How can I be free?" asked Badger.

"Don't take the ground for granted," said Raven.

# Honor

One evening Porcupine asked, "What is the place of honor in the practice?"

Raven said, "To be truly Porcupine takes practice."

Porcupine asked, "Come on, Rōshi, you don't mean just to be true to myself!"

Raven said, "To everybody else."

# EVERYDAY LIFE

Raccoon visited again from Cedarford and said, "My problem is how to use my practice in everyday life."

Raven asked, "What is your practice?"

Raccoon said, "Lots of zazen."

Raven said, "You probably can't use it."

Raccoon asked, "Then what's the good of it?"

Raven said, "Zazen arises from vows; vows arise from an aspiration for realization; aspiration for realization arises from a profound sense of unsatisfactoriness; the profound sense of unsatisfactoriness arises from self-centered views. When you realize that Right Views are right for toads and centipedes, then your practice includes washing your meat."

Raccoon asked, "Then zazen's not central?"

Raven said, "The core."

# Doubt

One evening Woodpecker asked, "The term *doubt* seems to be used in an unusual way in our practice. How do you understand it?"

Raven said, "What's this?"

Woodpecker asked, "Well, what is it?"

Raven asked, "What is it?"

# THE BEST TURNING POINTS

Owl came forward one evening and called up to Raven on his perch, saying, "Jackrabbit Rōshi was the first teacher you met."

Raven said, "That's right."

Owl said, "I've heard he said the best turning points come out of your own situation. Did you ever hear him say such a thing?"

Raven said, "What's your situation?"

Owl swung his head from side to side.

Raven asked, "What turning points come from that?"

Owl hooted.

Raven said, "I'm not convinced."

# RECTIFIED

During snacktime one afternoon, Black Bear asked, "How can I realize enlightenment?"

Raven asked, "What do you mean by 'enlightenment'?"

Black Bear said, "You know what I mean."

Raven said, "Fix up your terms and your path is fixed up."

Black Bear asked, "How can I fix up my terms?"

Raven said, "Your own intimate terms."

# REALIZATION AND EQUANIMITY

In a private meeting Woodpecker asked, "Is realization the same as equanimity?"

Raven said, "Don't confuse the beaver with the dam."

Woodpecker asked, "What's equanimity?"

Raven said, "I'm not a very good teacher."

Woodpecker said, "Oh, come on!"

Raven said, "It's okay."

# THE GOAL

Gray Wolf made one of her rare visits to the circle, and after a talk by Raven she remarked, "The goal of practice seems to be just more practice."

Raven bobbed his head. "Well?"

Gray Wolf hesitated, and then asked, "So there's no end to it?"

Raven hopped down from his perch to a little hummock beside Gray Wolf, put his beak to her ear, and murmured, "Thank goodness."

# MUTUALLY DEPENDENT ARISING

Owl spoke up one evening during the question period and said, "It is clear to me that you don't think much of 'mutually dependent arising' in connection with the morning star case. Is it a questionable notion to begin with?"

Raven said, "When you hoot, the whole forest hoots."

"Mole doesn't hoot," said Owl.

"I duck," said Mole.

"There you go!" said Raven.

# ARE YOU READY?

After Raven's response to Mole, the community fell silent. Finally, Woodpecker spoke up: "A while back you said that the call of the dove defines us, and now you say that when Owl hoots, the whole forest hoots. I'm confused. Do the two sounds have different functions?"

Raven said, "When Owl hoots, the whole forest hoots. Are you ready to be defined?"

# COMPASSION

Mole spoke up after a long silence one evening and asked, "What's compassion?"

Raven said, "That's an inside story."

Mole asked, "Inside what?"

Raven said, "Stars on your fur."

# GRACE

Reverend Crane visited the circle one evening and asked, "What role does God have in our practice?"

Raven said, "None."

Crane said, "But the Bible says He concerns himself even with the sparrow's fall."

Raven said, "Does it say He intervenes?"

Crane asked, "What about grace?"

Raven said, "The east wind brings soft showers."

Porcupine murmured, "The ground gets wet."

There was a general silence. Then Woodpecker said, "We seem to talk a lot about Christianity these days."

Raven said, "We're not talking about Christianity."

# JEALOUS

Grouse sought out Raven privately and said, "Sometimes I feel jealous of other students who seem to understand things so much better than I do."

Raven said, "I'm not a very good teacher."

Grouse said, "I heard that you were saying that."

Raven said, "It's okay."

# FACING IN, FACING OUT

Raccoon visited again from Cedarford and asked, "Why do some Zen groups sit facing into the circle and some sit facing out?"

Raven looked around and asked, "Any other questions?"

Raccoon sat back and was silent.

# THE PROPER PRESENTATION

Grouse spoke up one evening and said, "Everybody else seems to know what is going on here, but I'm in the dark. What would be a proper presentation?"

Raven said, "Anything goes."

Grouse said, "I'm at a loss."

Raven said, "Ding, ding, dang, dang, bong, bong, clank, clank."

Grouse clucked.

Raven said, "Hey, Grouse, not bad."

# TO THE OTHER SHORE

One evening Woodpecker asked, "What does it mean to cross to the other shore?"

Raven said, "Flowers crowd the cliffs."

# WHAT IS THE WAY? (I)

The folks were sitting around one moonlit night, enjoying one another's company, when Woodpecker asked, "What is the Way?"

Raven said, "The Ancestors got up and stretched."

Woodpecker said, "Well, we do, too."

Raven nodded.

Woodpecker asked, "Then the Way is nothing special?"

Raven said, "I'll always remember this full-moon gathering."

Woodpecker said, "It's nice, but how is it special?"

Raven said, "The moon."

# Māra the Founder

Black Bear appeared one evening and said, "Tell me about Māra. I understand that he is the Great Destroyer."

Raven said, "The Great Founder."

Black Bear said, "That's what the Buddha Shākyamuni is called."

Raven said, "Yes, but he never learned to blow smoke from his ears."

# HIDE YOURSELF

One evening Wolverine appeared and said, "I've been thinking about hiding myself and fasting."

Raven kicked a twig at Wolverine and said, "Hide yourself in that."

Wolverine stepped behind Black Bear and said, "I'm hidden."

Raven said, "Piffle. You don't even dream of my meaning."

Wolverine was silent.

Woodpecker spoke up and said, "What is your meaning?"

Raven said, "Good question, Wolverine."

# LIBERATION

Helping Raven arrange flowers before a meeting, Woodpecker asked, "What's liberation?"

Raven said, "Another couple of daffodils on this side, I think."

Woodpecker said, "You're not answering my question."

Raven said, "Daffodils."

# Greed, Hatred, and Ignorance

Moose Rōshi said to his students, "Greed, hatred, and ignorance are themselves Buddha-nature."

On one of his visits, Raccoon asked Raven about this. Raven said, "Moose oughta know."

# MISTAKES

Grouse said, "I feel very nervous when I lead our recitation of the sutras."

Raven said, "Mistakes are part of the ritual."

# THE MORAL BASIS

Porcupine came by for another special meeting with Raven and asked, "Does Zen have a moral basis?"

Raven said, "None whatsoever."

Porcupine exclaimed, "Empty! Empty!"

Raven said, "That's not what the magpie would say."

Porcupine bowed down and touched her face to the ground. Raven asked, "Why do you bow?"

Porcupine said, "The magpie is bowing."

Raven put his beak to her ear and said, "See me after the talk tonight."

# VAST INDEED

Porcupine came to see Raven after the talk that night and said, "The Blue Planet is immensely vast, isn't it?"

Raven said, "It doesn't stop there."

Porcupine wept.

Raven said, "Vast indeed. Vast indeed."

# WHERE ARE THEY?

One evening Owl said, "When Brown Bear visited us, Gray Wolf asked him about the dedication of our sutras to the enlightenment of bushes and grasses. He said, 'They are very patient.' I've been musing about this for a long time, and I still don't know what to make of it."

Raven asked, "Where are they?"

Owl said, "Bushes and grasses? All around."

Raven said, "Like the moon and birds."

Owl said, "Stones and clouds."

Raven said, "Very good. Now, where are they?"

Owl hooted.

Raven said, "Yes! Yes! On that path."

# SHAKING THE TREE

Raven called a special meeting of the Tallspruce community to announce that Porcupine was to become a teacher. "Porcupine has shaken the old crabapple tree and brought down some tasty little fruits," he said solemnly. "She'll share them if you like."

Black Bear said, "I'm afraid I'll get poked with her quills."

Raven said, "That's the risk."

Mole said, "I'd like to hear from Porcupine."

Porcupine said, "Actually, I don't poke. You poke yourself."

Black Bear said, "How can I avoid poking myself?"

Porcupine said, "Don't mess with me."

# THE PARTY

Members were excited about Raven's announcement. Woodpecker said, "Let's have a party." So the next night everybody gathered for grubs and leavings to celebrate.

Mole asked, "How is it to be a new teacher, Porcupine?"

Porcupine said, "Not sure yet."

Owl said, "The Assembly Oak is glad."

Badger asked, "Come on, how can that be?"

Porcupine said, "I'm glad for Owl."

# FASCINATED

At a private meeting Grouse said, "I'm not sure that I am dedicated enough to my practice."

Raven said, "Never mind about being dedicated."

Grouse said, "The truth is, I haven't the foggiest idea of what the practice really is."

"Me, either," Raven said, "but aren't you curious?"

Grouse said, "Fascinated."

Raven said, "There you go."

# THE JOKE

Porcupine was foraging near Stillpond and met Mallard unexpectedly. "Porcupine!" exclaimed Mallard, "I've wanted to ask you about something. It almost seems that you and Raven have a secret understanding of some kind."

Porcupine said, "We know the same joke."

"Can you let me in on it?" asked Mallard.

"It really doesn't amount to much," said Porcupine.

"Tell me," demanded Mallard.

"Mallard!" Porcupine exclaimed. "You aren't listening!"

## Guided by Karma

Wolverine wandered by again and positioned himself in the tall grass just outside the circle. "I don't know why I'm here," he said, with a rather faraway look in his eyes. "I guess my karma brought me."

Raven asked, "Don't you have a say-so?"

Wolverine said, "I just let myself be guided."

Raven said, "How about when a hunter trails meat to a trap?"

Wolverine put his head on his paws.

# Watch Out!

Cougar's presence created a certain tension in the circle, but he didn't seem aware of it. One evening he asked, "If all things pass quickly away, why should we be concerned about the suffering of others?"

Mole abruptly excused himself with a bow and hurried off, muttering. Raven said, "Māra can quote sutras."

Cougar said, "I'm serious."

Raven said, "All things pass quickly away."

# Impermanence

One night, under the starry sky, the circle was quiet and members seemed pensive. Badger broke the silence and said, "You know, I can't visualize myself expiring completely."

Raven said, "A ghost."

Badger said, "Even ghosts are impermanent, aren't they?"

Raven said, "Take care of your miseries now, and they won't abide."

# THE SEED OF ENLIGHTENMENT

Reverend Crane stopped by again one evening to hear one of Raven's talks. Afterward he asked, "Do I have the seed of enlightenment?"

Raven said, "You can be your best Reverend Crane."

Crane said, "Are we talking about character development?"

Raven said, "Have to start somewhere."

Crane said, "Maybe my best Crane is just something I imagine."

Raven said, "Have to start somewhere."

# THE DUALISTIC IDEA

Owl came to Raven for a private meeting and asked, "Is there something pure and clear underneath everything?"

Raven said, "You can say that."

Owl said, "Isn't it a dualistic idea? I thought Buddhism is a religion of oneness."

Raven croaked and then said, "Show me your essential purity and clarity."

Owl said, "I was just asking a question about Buddhism."

Raven said, "Don't neglect your religion of oneness."

# SELF AND SOUL

Owl spoke up again that evening after zazen and said, "The Buddha Shākyamuni said there is no self and no soul, yet I hear a lot of talk about essential nature, which sounds a lot like soul."

Raven said, "No self, no soul, no essential nature."

Owl said, "How come we hear so much talk about it?"

Raven said, "No excuse whatsoever."

# THE VOID

One evening Woodpecker asked, "What's the void?"
Raven said, "Not the void."

Woodpecker asked, "It's not really empty?"

Raven said, "The truth is, I really don't know."

# How to Die

One evening toward the end of a meeting, Mole said, "I've heard that Zen is for old folks to teach them how to die. What do you think of that notion?"

Raven said, "It helps young folks that way, too."

Mole asked, "They might have a fatal accident?"

Raven said, "I'm all for accidents."

# REBIRTH

Owl asked, "What do you think of the doctrine of reincarnation?"

Raven said, "Not my body."

Owl said, "Maybe my terminology is mistaken. What do you think of the doctrine of rebirth?"

Raven said, "Not my beak."

# Purpose

Badger confronted Raven after an early morning of zazen and asked, "What is the purpose of your practice?"

Raven said, "Having fun."

Badger said, "Having fun? You work hard and teach from morning to night. You never take a vacation."

Raven said, "Vacate."

# TRUE TEACHING

One evening Owl asked, "How can you tell whether a teaching is true or false?"

Raven said, "Moss on the rocks dries out when the creek is low."

Owl asked, "Good teaching is always wet?"

Raven said, "Sopping."

# WHERE IS THE BUDDHA?

Reverend Crane came to a meeting once again and asked, "Do Buddhists pray?"

Raven asked, "To whom?"

Crane said, "Well, to the Buddha Shākyamuni, I suppose."

Raven asked, "Where is the Buddha Shākyamuni?"

Crane said, "Where is he? Can you identify his place?"

Raven said, "For sure. Just like anyone."

Crane said, "Well, I'm like anyone, and I can identify my place. That really doesn't answer the question."

Raven said, "It's all it takes."

# EVERYTHING COLLAPSED

Wolverine dropped by for zazen and announced, "Everything on the Blue Planet is contained in this appearance."

Porcupine said, "That's true. How do you maintain it?"

Wolverine hesitated.

Porcupine said, "The Blue Planet collapsed."

# MOCKINGBIRD

One fine day Mockingbird met Raven on the Assembly Oak and asked, "Who is Raven Rōshi?"

Raven held out his wings. Mockingbird held out her wings. Raven croaked. Mockingbird croaked.

Raven abruptly pecked at her claw, and she tumbled from the tree.

# FLIGHTY

Woodpecker asked, "What is truth?"

Raven said, "Clouds gather over Rockysummit."

Woodpecker said, "Seems very ordinary."

Raven said, "Yesterday an arrow flew past Stag Sensei and went clear across the creek."

Woodpecker said, "He must have been scared."

Raven said, "Flighty!"

# SWITCH ROLES

Gray Wolf said, "Why do we always do everything in exactly the same way?"

Raven said, "Steady on."

Gray Wolf said, "Maybe we should switch roles sometimes. Somebody else could be the teacher and you could be just one of the students."

Raven said, "It's happening."

# RISKS

Porcupine came to consult with Raven and said, "I'm beginning to see the risks in being a teacher."

Raven said, "They're built in."

Porcupine asked, "How do you cope?"

Raven drew himself up and said, "Don't accuse me of coping!"

# Too Soon

Woodpecker asked, "When Brown Bear said you should camp out for a while, was there anything underlying his words?"

Raven said, "Woodpecker!"

Woodpecker said, "Yes?"

Raven hung his head and turned away, saying, "Ah, too soon."

# LOVE

Mole spoke up one evening and asked, "Why don't we ever talk about love in our discussions?"

Raven asked, "What would you like to say about love?"

Mole stared back at Raven and was silent.

# BOWING

Gray Wolf spoke up after zazen one evening and said, "Isn't it undignified to bow before the Buddha? I always feel rather humiliated."

Raven said, "Not enough."

# THE TRAIN

Wolverine spoke up during the question period one evening and said, "I am finally in touch with my essential nature. It has been hidden all this time."

Raven said, "Is that so? Well, well."

Wolverine said, "It's my basic nature, the source of my inspiration."

Raven said, "My, my."

Wolverine said, "It's beyond all ideas of life and death."

Porcupine said, "More like the train beyond Cedarford."

Mole asked, "What do you mean?"

Porcupine said, "It never seems to break down."

Wolverine put his head on his paws.

Next day, Woodpecker spoke to Owl about this. "I thought

Porcupine was bristly toward Wolverine last night," he said.

"Yes," said Owl, "Porcupine was being Porcupine. But you know, Wolverine did break down at last."

# INTELLIGENCE

During a question period, Mole asked, "How important is intelligence to the practice?"

Raven asked, "How do you use it?"

Mole said, "As best I can with what it is."

Raven asked, "How do you depend on it?"

"You know," said Mole, "I really don't depend on it very much at all."

Raven bobbed his head silently.

# THE ACORN

Woodpecker asked, "Is there anything that can't be expressed in words?"

Raven said, "Nothing."

Woodpecker asked, "Even the ineffable experience of the Buddha under the Bodhi tree?"

Raven said, "The morning star."

Porcupine said, "There's a kernel in that acorn."

Woodpecker asked, "How can I get at it?"

Porcupine said, "Come on, Woodpecker! What's that chisel beak for?"

# ALL TRUTHS

Owl dropped by one afternoon and asked Raven, "I've heard that the opposite of truth is also true. What do you think of this idea?"

Raven said, "Let's have a snack."

Owl said, "Aren't you devaluing my question?"

Raven said, "Not at all. We have fresh grubs today."

# NON SEQUITUR

That evening Woodpecker asked, "I've heard that without Buddha there would be no dew on the grass. What do you think?"

Raven said, "Tonight we're all out of snacks."

Woodpecker said, "You're full of non sequiturs these days."

Raven said, "Ah, Woodpecker, you should talk."

# SAMENESS

Wolverine began attending meetings on a fairly regular basis, joining the circle instead of holding himself outside. One evening he asked, "If everything is essentially the same, how is it that winter follows fall, and spring follows winter?"

Raven said, "I defer to Porcupine."

Porcupine said, "I defer to Black Bear."

Wolverine said, "Black Bear? He's off snoozing until spring."

Porcupine said, "Well?"

Wolverine said nothing.

# THE SABBATH

After Porcupine's final response to Wolverine, Mole spoke up and said, "I have something quite different to ask about. My wife is not the least bit interested in our practice. Is there something I can do to encourage her?"

Raven asked, "What *does* interest her?"

Mole said, "She likes to go over to the Little Church in the Grotto and listen to the sermons."

Raven said, "Keep the Sabbath."

# POWER

Owl asked, "Does the Way have its own power?"

Raven said, "It circulates."

Owl asked, "What is its path of circulation?"

Raven said, "Why don't you lead the discussion tomorrow night?"

# THE WORD

Stag Sensei invited Raven to speak to his students, and Porcupine went along as his attendant. In their absence, Owl led the discussion but said very little.

Wolverine asked, "If truth is essentially wordless, why do we usually talk so much at these meetings?"

Woodpecker said, "Maybe we should listen to the silence between the words."

Hearing of this later, Porcupine said, "The word! The word!"

# Forgetting

Raccoon visited Raven from Cedarford once again, and Raven welcomed him, saying, "I'm sorry I don't have your kind of food to offer you."

Raccoon said, "No problem. I come for the Dharma anyway."

Raven said, "I don't have that, either."

Raccoon said, "Okay, okay. But maybe you can comment on something Moose Rōshi is saying these days. 'Forget to the bottom, and the bottom will serve you.'"

"I see his point," said Raven.

"How would you say it, Rōshi?"

"Forget to the robin, and the robin will serve you," said Raven.

# PORES

One day Badger came by for a private chat. "What is the source of compassion?" he asked.

"Pores," said Raven.

"How are pores the source of compassion?" asked Badger.

Raven said, "There are small pores in between the big ones."

Badger asked, "What do the pores do?"

Raven said, "There are littler pores in between the small ones."

Badger said, "And so on, I suppose."

Raven said, "Not much left, after all."

# MĀRA IS PRODDING

After this exchange about compassion, Badger said, "Well, I got my comeuppance on that one. I have another question—not really a question, more a confession. It's the one that's been on my mind for some time. I've sat with you all this time and not realized very much at all. I wake up in the night feeling guilty that I haven't made more of an effort. You devote yourself to us, and I feel that I've failed you."

Raven said, "Māra is prodding you."

Badger said, "It hurts."

Raven said, "It's the only way he knows."

# NOTIONS

Turkey spoke up one evening and said, "Listening to Grandma at Vinecot, I get the impression that all notions fall apart. What do you make of this?"

Raven said, "Nothing."

Turkey asked, "How about the Buddha?"

Raven said, "Bring him around."

Turkey asked, "Then what are we about?"

Raven glanced at Porcupine, and both exclaimed, "Buddha!"

# UPHILL

Wolverine asked, "Do you practice going with the flow?"
Raven asked, "Is that a practice?"
Wolverine asked, "What is practice?"
Raven said, "Going against the grain."
Wolverine asked, "Sounds hard."
Raven said, "Uphill."

# THE ANCESTORS

One evening Gray Wolf came by after a long absence and asked, "Are the old masters of the past really our own ancestors?"

Raven said, "Most certainly."

Gray Wolf said, "But it seems that they were folks who wore clothes."

Raven said, "I can't answer for the dream."

# Zazen

The next evening Gray Wolf attended the circle gathering again and asked, "After all, what is zazen?"

Raven said, "Animal practice."

Gray Wolf said, "Of course it's animal practice; I wouldn't suppose that stones and trees do it."

Raven said, "That would be the zazen of stones and trees."

# The Poem

Wolverine approached Raven after a meeting had broken up and said, "I've composed a poem about my practice. Do you want to hear it?"

Raven said, "No."

Wolverine said, "I'm going to recite it anyway."

Raven gave a croak and flew up into the Assembly Oak.

Next day, Mole told Porcupine about this and said, "I thought Rōshi was pretty rude to Wolverine. Why did he make such a point of not wanting to hear his poem?"

Porcupine said, "He already knew it by heart."

# What Is the Way? (II)

Copperhead came by one evening unannounced. Mole made himself scarce, and Owl, Woodpecker, and Grouse set up a clatter. Copperhead said, "Excuse me, everybody. I came for the Great Law, not for my dinner." The birds quieted down, but Mole did not return.

Raven asked, "Do you have a question?"

"Yes," said Copperhead. "I'm really interested in the Way, but I don't seem to have the right livelihood for it."

Raven said, "The Way does not depend on your livelihood."

Copperhead asked, "What is the Way?"

Raven said, "We'd be totally lost without you."

# PAINFUL

The next night Woodpecker said to Raven, "You told Copperhead that we'd be totally lost without him. Well, speak for yourself, Rōshi. He eats my babies. And don't tell me the stars don't care. I've heard that one."

Raven said, "Painful."

# Affectionate Acceptance

In a private encounter with Raven, Badger said, "I confess that after all this time, I feel very impatient with my zazen."

Raven said, "That's okay."

Badger said, "I have the feeling that if I weren't so anxious, I might get somewhere."

Raven said, "Affectionate acceptance is the way of all the Ancestors."

# ANGUISH

Raven took his perch on the Assembly Oak and said, "The Buddha said that anguish has a source. How would you identify that source?"

Wolverine said, "I know that one. The source of anguish is clinging."

Raven said, "What if the forest burned down?"

Wolverine said, "I might feel liberated."

Raven bowed his head and murmured, "Oh, well . . . congratulations."

# SERENE

Owl came for a private interview and said, "Sometimes when I sit, the whole forest is quiet. Everything is still and serene."

Raven said, "That's really nice."

Owl said, "Is there anything more?"

Raven said, "You know what happens."

Owl said, "The trout jumps after the fly."

Raven said, "Exactly."

# Pushing

Badger asked, "Do you think it is important to sit up all night when we feel especially deep in the practice?"

Raven said, "Blackberries ripen in August."

Badger said, "We shouldn't push it?"

Raven said, "Let it push you."

# THE RIGHT PATH

B lack Bear asked, "Am I on the right path?"

Raven said, "Of course. Wolverine is on the right path."

Black Bear said, "Wolverine? He seems pretty far afield."

Raven said, "His path."

# TEACHING

One day the group was sitting around having a snack when Woodpecker asked, "After all this time, how would you sum up your teaching?"

Raven said, "Try some of these tree borers. They're quite tasty."

Woodpecker said, "Is that your teaching, Rōshi?"

Raven said, "Teaching."

# Talking about It

One evening Owl spoke up first during the question period and asked, "Is there anything we can't talk about?"

Raven said, "We can't talk about anything."

Owl asked, "Aren't we doing it now?"

Raven said, "It disappeared."

Owl asked, "How can we retain it?"

Raven said, "It's not a matter of retaining. Speak!"

Owl was silent.

# THE BEST PRESENTATION

Porcupine met with Raven in private one afternoon and asked, "What is the best presentation of the great matter?"

Raven said, "The thing."

Porcupine asked, "How do you present the thing?"

Raven said, "Splash."

# What the Practice Teaches

Gray Wolf dropped by again and asked, "What can the practice teach me?"

Raven said, "What you already know."

Gray Wolf asked, "What do I already know?"

Raven said, "You're dying."

Gray Wolf said, "I try not to think about it."

Raven said, "Not thinking about it is okay."

Gray Wolf said, "But there it is."

Raven said, "There it is."

After a short silence, Woodpecker asked, "Isn't there a moment of understanding that seems to change everything?"

Raven said, "Day to night."

Woodpecker asked, "What does that moment teach me?"

Raven said, "The Assembly Oak."

Woodpecker said, "But I knew about that before."

Raven said, "Like I said."

# THE UNDERLYING SCHEME

Porcupine, conferring with Raven privately, asked, "What if a student asks about the underlying scheme of things—how would you respond?"

Raven said, "It's cooler tonight. It'll rain tomorrow."

Porcupine said, "Sometimes it rains after a hot spell."

Raven said, "We'll all take shelter with Mole and his family."

# SAVED

Woodpecker said, "We don't have a very big member-ship—not like Stag Sensei's group. Their place is so crowded with folks that they're talking about enlarging it. What can we do to attract more members?"

Raven said, "The Blue Planet is only so big."

Woodpecker asked, "But what about our vow to save everybody?"

Raven said, "I don't want to be saved."

# WEIRD

Mallard flew in one evening and reported, "Miners keep coming to Beaverdam to wash for gold. I think that's a pretty weird activity."

Raven said, "Magpies wouldn't think so."

Mallard said, "Magpies are weird."

Raven said, "The foresters are closing in, too."

# THE MEMORIAL SERVICE

Badger's little daughter Furry was caught by Cougar and eaten. The Badger family went into mourning, and the community held a memorial service. Folks came forward and offered flowers at the altar and spoke. Cougar did not attend.

While folks were eating grubs and leavings after the service, Mole said to Badger, "I grieve at your loss, and I'm deeply upset with Cougar. To think that a member of our own community could do such a thing."

Badger said, "He didn't know. And I eat baby mice, after all."

Mole said, "Over at the Little Church in the Grotto they say the lion shall lie down with the lamb."

Raven sighed and said, "The raven, too."

Wolverine said, "I need my meat. I can't imagine just eating grains and fruits like some of the birds around here."

Raven said, "Bushes and grasses are even slower."

# CONFIDENCE

Grouse came by one day for a private talk with Raven. She said, "My problem is that I have no confidence."

Raven said, "Aren't you quieter these days?"

Grouse said, "Yes, I guess I am."

Raven said, "There you go."

Grouse said, "I guess I can do it."

Raven said, "It's total silence that removes all doubt."

# ZAZEN FOR THE YOUNG ONES

One evening Badger asked, "Do you encourage the young ones to do zazen?"

Raven asked, "What happens when they see you sit down to practice?"

Badger said, "They go out to play."

Raven said, "Well?"

Badger said, "Maybe I can do something now, and later they will remember and take up the practice."

Raven said, "Bow."

# Last Will and Testament

Mole and Woodpecker came together to see Raven one afternoon. Mole said, "Woodpecker and I have been noticing that you're getting on in years and wondering—have you made your last will and testament?"

Raven said, "Thank you."

The three of them sat together silently for a while. Then Woodpecker asked, "Looking back, is there anything you would like to have done differently?"

Raven said, "How could I?"

Mole asked, "Each time you decided which way to go. Are you sorry about any of those decisions?"

Raven said, "How could I?"

# WISE COUNSEL

Mole continued pressing Raven. "How would you like to be remembered?"

Raven said, "If you can forget yourself even once, then I can be forgotten."

Mole said, "I learned with my mother's milk that if I forget myself even once, something will consume me."

Raven said, "Wise counsel. Wise counsel."

# FORESTERS

Owl spoke up the next evening and said, "I've been brooding about your remark to Mallard that the foresters are closing in. I think we aren't facing things. It's always been hard to find food and raise a family, but now the forest is shrinking and folks like Wolverine can't even find a mate."

Raven said, "Yes."

Owl said, "I feel despair about those foresters."

Woodpecker interrupted and said, "The problem is that they aren't really foresters."

Raven said, "Yes."

Owl asked, "What can be done?"

Raven did not respond, and the group was silent. Finally Porcupine said, "Their children will remember us."

Owl said, "Small comfort."

Raven said, "Brontosaur lives."

# Taking Over

Raven called Porcupine for a private meeting. "It'll soon be time for me to be moving on. Are you up for taking over?"

Porcupine said, "It won't be Raven Zen."

Raven asked, "What kind of Zen will it be?"

Porcupine said, "Don't touch."

Raven said, "Exactly. Exactly."

# MOVING ON

Raven took his perch on the Assembly Oak and addressed a special meeting of the Tallspruce community, saying, "It's time for me to be moving on."

Porcupine asked, "Where will you be going?"

Raven said, "Where cedar roots stand bare in the creek."

A hush fell over the circle. Grouse could be heard sniffling. At last Porcupine asked, "Do you have any last words for us?"

Raven said, "Trust."

# ACKNOWLEDGMENTS

Thanks to Nelson Foster for his developmental editing and his gracious foreword, and to Jennifer Rain Crosby for her endearing illustrations. Thanks to Phil Vinson for a key suggestion.

# NOTES

1. There are two versions of the Buddha's realization story in the Mahāyāna tradition. The first, in which the Buddha exclaims "Now I see that all beings are the Tathāgata. Only their delusions and preoccupations keep them from realizing that fact!" is derived from the *Hua-yen ching*. See Thomas Cleary, *The Flower Ornament Scripture*, 3 vols. (Boulder, Colo.: Shambhala, 1984–1987), II: 314–15. The other version is derived from Dogen Kigen's *Hotsumujōshin (Developing the Supreme Mind)*, which has the Buddha exclaim, "At this moment, I and all beings have attained the Way!" See Gudo Nishijima and Chodo Cross, *Master Dogen's Shobogenzo*, 4 vols. (Woking, Surrey, U.K.: Windbell Publications, 1994–1999), III: 259.

2. "Mutually dependent arising" is the notion that each being appears contingent on others and other events, and there is no central essence, self, or soul. This is a view developed by the Buddha Shākyamuni and is found throughout Buddhism. See

the early chapters of Dale S. Wright, *Philosophical Meditations on Zen Buddhism* (New York: Cambridge University Press, 2000).

3. Prairie Dog seems to be extrapolating from the notion of mutually dependent arising to the concept of an underlying structure of some kind.

4. I like to think that Brown Bear is echoing Stevenson:

> The children sing in far Japan,
> The children sing in Spain;
> The organ with the organ man
> Is singing in the rain.

Robert Louis Stevenson, *A Child's Garden of Verses* (New York: Charles Scribner's Sons, 1905), 13.

5. *Zazen* is the seated practice of focused inquiry and attunement, originally a Sino-Japanese term.

6. "Turning points" refers to kōans, themes of Zen practice to be made clear.

7. *Mu* is the Japanese pronunciation (and probably the ancient Chinese pronunciation) of the Chinese word meaning "no; does not have." It is found in the story "A monk asked Chao-chou in all earnestness, 'Has the dog Buddha-nature or not?' Chao-chou said, '*Mu*.'" This is often the first case taken up in Zen study. See Robert Aitken, *The Gateless Barrier: The Wu-men kuan (Mumonkan)* (San Francisco: North Point, 1990), 7.

8. Raven is echoing a Zen Buddhist folk story about the Buddha and Indra, emperor of the gods: "When the Buddha was walking with his disciples, he pointed to the ground and said, 'This spot would be a good place to build a sanctuary.' Indra took a blade of grass, stuck it into the ground, and said, 'The sanctuary is built.' The Buddha smiled." See Thomas Cleary, *Book of Serenity* (Hudson, N.Y.: Lindisfarne, 1990), 17.

9. See note 1.

10. Porcupine's question is reminiscent of the stock question in Zen literature, "What is the reason Bodhidharma came from the West?" See D. T. Suzuki, *Essays in Zen Buddhism: Second Series* (New York: Samuel Weiser, 1976), pp. 225–53.

11. Woodpecker, with her interest in terminology, had already picked up on the expression "appropriate means" (*upāya* in Sanskrit), a reference to the way of teaching that fits the time, place, and the person involved.

12. Bodhidharma (d. 532) is thought to have brought Dhyāna Buddhism from India to China, establishing it as Ch'an (Zen), and is also thought to have founded such martial arts as karate.

13. Owl would seem to be quoting Dōgen Kigen. See *Sokushin Sokubutsu* (*This Very Mind Is Buddha*) in Nishijima and Cross, *Master Dogen's Shobogenzo,* I: 58.

14. Here Owl seems to be quoting Huang-po. See John Blofeld, *The Zen Teachings of Huang Po* (New York: Grove, 1958), 29.

15. Badger is speaking here as a true student of Raven and his predecessors, who stress the unity of all Buddhism. The Eightfold

Path is central to classical Buddhism and is not featured so much in the Mahāyāna. See Walpola Rahula, *What the Buddha Taught* (New York: Grove, 1959), 45–50.

16. The idea that bushes and grasses have Buddha-nature and are on the path to nirvana is a persistent idea in Japanese Buddhism and is much argued. See William LaFleur, trans., *Mirror for the Moon: A Selection of Poems by Saigyo (1118–1190)* (New York: New Directions, 1978), xvii–xviii. See also Jamie Hubbard and Paul L. Swanson, eds., *Pruning the Bodhi Tree: The Storm over Critical Buddhism* (Honolulu: University of Hawaii Press, 1997), 3–4.

17. Mallard refers to the "Four Bodhisattva Vows," or "Great Vows for All," which Mahāyāna Buddhist students have recited for fifteen centuries:

> The many beings are numberless, I vow to save them;
> Greed, hatred, and ignorance rise endlessly, I vow to
>     abandon them;
> Dharma gates are countless, I vow to wake them;
> Buddha's way is unsurpassed, I vow to embody it fully.

See Robert Aitken, *Encouraging Words: Zen Buddhist Teachings for Western Students* (New York: Pantheon, 1993), 172.

18. For the traditional version of the words of Hui-neng, the Sixth Ancestor (638–713), see Philip B. Yampolsky, *The Platform Sutra of the Sixth Patriarch: The Text of the Tun-huang Manuscript* (New York: Columbia University Press, 1967), 143.

19. Raven echoes old Zen stories and Wu-men's comments about the staffs of Zen personages. See Cases 43 and 44 of the *Wu-men kuan* in Aitken, *The Gateless Barrier*, 261–68.

20. Raven is quoting the *Heart Sutra:* see Aitken, *Encouraging Words*, 173.

21. See note 17.

22. I like to think that Raven is echoing Bashō:

> Ah, how glorious!
> The young leaves, the green leaves,
> Glittering in the sunshine!

R. H. Blyth, trans., *Haiku*, 4 vols. (Tokyo: Hokuseido, 1949–1952), III: 278.

23. "Middle Way" can refer to the Way of the Buddha, harmonizing such opposites as the particular and the universal. It also can refer to the Eightfold Path.

24. Compare Raven's words with those of Keats in his admonition to Shelley, "Load every rift of your subject with ore." Robert Pack, ed., *Selected Letters of John Keats* (New York: New American Library, 1974), 229.

# INDEX OF KOANS

Zen Master Raven

Index of Koans

# ABOUT THE AUTHOR

Robert Aitken was one of the most prominent, influential, and highly esteemed Zen masters of the twentieth century. He was of seminal importance in shaping the expression of modern American Zen and, as one of the original founders of the Buddhist Peace Fellowship, was also a leading social activist advocating for social justice of all varieties. He is the author of numerous books on Zen Buddhism, including *Taking the Path of Zen*, *Mind of Clover*, *The Practice of Perfection*, and *Original Dwelling Place*. He died in 2010.

# About Wisdom Publications

Wisdom Publications is the leading publisher of classic and contemporary Buddhist books and practical works on mindfulness. To learn more about us or to explore our other books, please visit our website at wisdompubs.org or contact us at the address below.

Wisdom Publications
199 Elm Street
Somerville, MA 02144 USA

We are a 501(c)(3) organization, and donations in support of our mission are tax deductible.

Wisdom Publications is affiliated with the Foundation for the Preservation of the Mahayana Tradition (FPMT).